RAINDROPS OF PAIN

ANTHOLOGY

SUJISHA SUBRAHMANIAN

Copyright © Sujisha Subrahmanian
All Rights Reserved.

ISBN 978-1-68523-016-6

This book has been published with all efforts taken to make the material error-free after the consent of the author. However, the author and the publisher do not assume and hereby disclaim any liability to any party for any loss, damage, or disruption caused by errors or omissions, whether such errors or omissions result from negligence, accident, or any other cause.

While every effort has been made to avoid any mistake or omission, this publication is being sold on the condition and understanding that neither the author nor the publishers or printers would be liable in any manner to any person by reason of any mistake or omission in this publication or for any action taken or omitted to be taken or advice rendered or accepted on the basis of this work. For any defect in printing or binding the publishers will be liable only to replace the defective copy by another copy of this work then available.

Co-authors & My Friends

Contents

Foreword — vii
Preface — ix
Acknowledgements — xi

1. Your Memories Are All I Have — 1
2. My Heartbeat Says — 3
3. Broken Heart — 5
4. Unheard Voices — 6
5. Need Is Not Love And Love Is Not Need — 7
6. My Love In Pain... — 8
7. Unconditional Love With Pain — 11
8. Diaries Of Love — 12
9. Pain In Love — 13
10. Somethings Ought To Be Just Loved — 15
11. Desolated Me — 16
12. It Is Hard To Tell! — 18
13. What If It Hurts? — 20
14. An Afflicted Story — 22
15. Joyful Pain — 23
16. Heavens Seems To Be Cry...! — 25
17. The One That Got Away — 27
18. A Letter To My Love – — 29
19. Where I Am All Alone — 30
20. Red — 31
21. Yes There Is Pain In Love — 33

Contents

22. I Can Win Every Sword	34
23. Beauty Of The Mother's Love	35
24. Pain In Rain	37
Introdusing Co-authors	39
Compiler	45

Foreword

This book is a collection of poems. The authors and the editor have tried best to edit and curate the write-ups and is made plagiarism free.

Preface

"My soul is pure magic
 Think about yours
 You feel the same."
 _ Sujisha Subrahmanian

Acknowledgements

First of all, I would like to thank God for giving me the blessings to complete this Anthology.

My parents and my Sister, for always inspiring and encouraging me to achieve all victories in my life.

I would like to thank all my co-authors. Without their support and participation this Anthology wouldn't be successful.

I thank each and every one who worked behind this Anthology and made this as a wonderful one. I am eternally grateful to all the writers who are the part of this Anthology.

I specially thank Notion Press and the entire team, for their support and help through this Journey.

Heartily thanks to 'Xpress Publishing, and my Guide Ms. Yamini Shekar, for believing in me.

CHAPTER ONE

Your memories are all I have

Dancing in the blossoms of you,
I came across a life so new.
Why are the scents getting faded away,
And your memories are all I have!

Losing myself into your hands,
I perfectly found where love stands.
Why am i getting solitary again,
and your memories are all I have!

Filling myself with the dreams of you,
I found my world with an adorable view.
Why are my eyes getting empty of them,
and your memories are all I have!

Making glories with you in a walk,
I discussed each of them in our every single talk.
Why are there only silence again,
and your memories are all I have!

Finding ways to get near your heart,

I met myself who was somewhere apart.
Why am I losing myself again,
and your memories are all I have!

Keeping your memories somewhere in my heart,
I survived this life but never made a new start.
Just don't take my beats apart,
because your memories are all I have!
Your memories are all I have!

-Iqra Hameed

CHAPTER TWO

My heartbeat says

My heartbeat says,
    You are my true friend,
    there is nothing else I seek from the world.
    Though I am not mentioned your name here because
    I don't think I have to express my friendship is royal.
    You know that how much I love you,
    what's your value in my life!
    I know there's a misunderstanding but it lived for
    Short period because we trust each other.
    My journey is with you.
    Where do I want to go?
    I want to spend my life with you.
    Don't stay away from me even for a moment.
    You teach me a path to ride,
    I know you have a personal life with your special one,
    but still you guide me in my way.
    You changed my life for good,
    by embracing me...
    you put me on the sky,
    picking me up from a cot...O friend,
    I considered your friendship
    my god.this is the prayer of my heart
    that you never go far from me.

when I have to live without you,
such a day should never come.
where can one find a friend like you
where are there such friendships...
where one is not showing love, affection, care etcs,
but there's one who always want the support behind it.
This is a weird friend's friendship.
It's you and just you.
You're there in every smile of mine.
You're there in every moment and in every year.
You're there in my sorrow and in my joy.
O my friend, your friendship will be with me forever.
You find happiness from all my pain.
You are the reason of my smile.
You understand my past, believe in me!!
It's enough for me to rebuild my self again.
You are far away from my eyes, not from my hearts.
You're my friend, my best friend.
I can't just live with out you.
I love you the most.
But in case of love you left me gave me memories
but that pain I can't bear.
Sometimes there's fault in our stars.
Sometimes there's fault in their stars.
And there is my fault that you are not with me.
  _ Swapna S. Tripathy

CHAPTER THREE

Broken Heart

Believing every word you ever uttered
Doing what you liked best everytime.
Trusting every lie you told for days
Changing myself for your wishes
Laughing at your jokes from dawn to dusk
Thinking the best moments of my life.
Never imagining I will consider you my biggest mistake.
You are the one who broke my heart.
Yes you are the greatest regret of my life
Not because you lied and cheated
Because I believed you everytime.
Even when everyone said not to trust you
Even though my soul told not to trust you.
Eventually the truth comes into light
I realise my mistake and try to move on
But a heart broken cannot be so easily mended
With time things will change with time I will forgive you.
　_ HARSHITA VERMA

CHAPTER FOUR

Unheard Voices

She cried, she fought,
with her mind's darkest thoughts.
She loved, she cared a lot,
but in return got what?
He abused and gave wound,
to the girl he himself found.
She tolerated everything,
still said nothing.
She lost herself in his love,
she got no one to really speak of.
All alone in her dark life,
his words cut her deep like a knife.
Sometimes the love of your life won't listen your voices,
as this life and love goes on with choices.
_ Pragya Verma

CHAPTER FIVE

Need is not Love And Love is not need

Need is not Love And Love is not need.
    These are two different things.
    Need means you want something.
    But Love means You expect
    something unexpectedly and undoubtedly.
    There is a Special place And
    There is someone's special place.
    Life without love is like a tree
    without blossoms or fruit.
    Love recognizes no barriers.
    It jumps hurdles, leaps fences,
    penetrates walls to arrive at
    its destination full of hope.
    The real lover is the man who can
    thrill you by kissing your forehead or
    smiling into your eyes or just staring into space.
    _ Swapna S. Tripathy

CHAPTER SIX

My Love in Pain...

How long has it been,
    Since you disappeared.
    I'm walking through time,
    That's been laid out .
    I'm embracing all my pain and laughter inside,
    The seasons get busier..
    The landscapes changed,
    But your memories are engraved in my heart.
    Whenever I think of you,
    Suddenly, I get lost,
    Like waking up from a long dream,
    My overwhelming heart tells me,
    I'm trapped within your heart...
    You started to stay with my tears,
    I'm losing myself,
    You made me lose everything in your love,
    I'm still tired,
    You made me see the world in your eyes,
    Even a sad sigh is hard to exhale .
    A day that end with tears,
    Is where I am today.
    I don't know if time's flowing,
    I'm getting scared all day.

Holding on to the constant loneliness,
Dreams of you are like mirage,
Even if I try to erase it with my tears,
Everything is shattered.
I'm still hanging on irreversible memories..
After all my dreams that
I couldn't fullfill,my heart has been torn apart.
My life is lost,
My hope is lost,
My light is lost,
The time I can't feel again,
Is the last memory I have...
In the midst of the cold breeze,
I said my wish,
If I can go to your side ,
My days in endless pain won't be too difficult.
Even if I could only see you,
My thick memories were fading,
My love is alone,
My love is trapped inside you....
I know that,
This wound in my heart will bleed again,
Now, I'm far away from the one I love.
I can see that,
You're in love with someone else.
But I don't know what to do,
There is no easy way of letting go.
But, I Know there's no sense,
In holding on too much to something fading.
You're so happy,
Deep inside , I just don't know how to feel.
It's not easy for me to letting you go.
And somehow, I'll try to get you off my mind..

RAINDROPS OF PAIN

Only sad rain falls outside the window,
I feel so sad,
Because I can't ever see you again.
You are moving on your life,
The light in your eyes,
Starts to fade.
No way of going back,
The way it used to be,
I took away your pain with me,
Now I say,
Death today feels alright.
We're heading for an ending,
And your mind is full of doubt,
Look at your life today,
When will it fade away.
Now,
The light in your eyes started to fade away...
_ Sheena Catherine

CHAPTER SEVEN

Unconditional Love With Pain

From starting to end
    I accepted your flaws
    And loved each other.
    When I raised any questions
    You just asked me to "Don't ask"
    And showered tons of love
    I believed in you
    But you cheated me
    And beg me not to leave.
    I asked for our wedding date,
    You gave your child
    And said "I don't want children"
    To kill or give baby to orphanage.
    Moment I came to know
    About your Cancer,
    Our baby grown up with my friends.
    We together can fight against cancer
    But your ego
    Made you to destroy yourself
    And left me and baby alone!
    -Sakthidevi. J

CHAPTER EIGHT

Diaries of love

A lot of twists in a tale,
    Is it love or affection?
    You came like firefly and gave me light
    Thrown away my darkness.
    I believed you were there,
    I believed you more than me
    Days had passed,
    Will our feelings remain the same
    For the years you told.
    The love I've on you
    Will remain forever!
    Will you give me the hope
    That will be by my side
    For countless years.
    I never knew I would fall for you,
    I never easily believed others
    But I believed you the most.
    There was no silence between us,
    We had only laughter's and happiness.
    But now the silence kills me
    And I'm losing myself in searching you
    From the places we had our memories of love.
    _ Anushiya. B

CHAPTER NINE

Pain In Love

Love, expected feeling but still unexpected happens,
We search it for happiness but our mind saddens.
It brings us together and so we can be separated,
By creating random illusion which is anonymously animated.
We feel nothing, but feel something,
That something made us to realize we are in love thing.
But that something is a painful thing,
Because we failed to realize we felt nothing.
Love is like dancing in the fire and singing in the air.
Though it burns, we love to dance,
Though it's hollow, we love to sing.
How I feel about love?
The meaning of life? No.
It is a morning sleep under a warm blanket
Of cold old days.
We want to wakeup but the heart says,
"Sleep more, feel the pleasure".
No work pressure is important than love pleasure.
The warmth that we get under the love blanket is pleasure,
But later we will realize it's just for leisure.
Being in love is like sleeping eternally,

So, love is a blanket.
It will mesmerize us with the warmth,
And tells us to sleep at the time of wrath.
You want to sleep there eternally but you can't sleep there forever,
That's the pain in love.
Love is a painful life behind a mask,
I wonder how many people are hiding behind that mask.
Love is like a deceived comrade that suck out our energy.
You can't help it, you can't tolerate the sufferings,
But you love to do it.
We think love is the power to control all the sufferings,
But it is the pain that adds up more sufferings.
If our heart knows that we will end up alone,
Then we won't look for love,
Then we won't look for pain.
But understand there is no pain in love,
Because love itself is a pain.
-L. Caroline Felicita

CHAPTER TEN

Somethings ought to be Just loved

Somethings ought to be just loved
Nevertheless its painfull but you still embrace the pain,
You make an effort to move on but all in vain,
You try hard to unlove and free yourselves from feelings but you end up falling .

The pain you feel when efforts are not mutual,
The pain when you are the only one loving and the other is brutal,
Hard ,right? The nights you spent talking each others soul,
Rememberance of that just meant to you and to them it was no more.

If there is love ,there would b pain amd insecurity,
You deal with it or just leave it focusing on priorities,
You love because you know how painful it is to be unloved by the loved one,
So now you try to move on because you know how dreadful the pain in love is!!!
　_ Chakshu pahuja

CHAPTER ELEVEN

Desolated Me

Every relationship ends in pain,
    My thoughts get some oscillation
    This is because of a cause,
    But now I am desolate...
    Once upon a time,
    You were me and I were you
    My desire is to sustain the same,
    But now I am desolate...
    The first sight that made me lose
    I never dismiss those memories
    Since that is my treasure,
    But now I am desolate...
    You occupied my heart at day, noon, and night
    Your hope nestled me so tight
    And that was a beautiful tragedy,
    But now I am desolate...
    Life with you was priceless
    A day without you is aimless
    I wondered at the love hate relationship
    But now I am desolate...
    My sweetest devotion is only for you
    My toughest emotion is only because of you
    This is because I love you,

But now I am desolate...
Who will take care of my broken heart?
Who will make me feel so comfort?
To whom will I share all my emotions?
That's way now I am desolate...
Your job is your first love
So I am alone with our lovable dove
I wish to be with you for twenty four hours,
No more I want to be desolate...
_ B. Nishanthini

CHAPTER TWELVE

It is hard to tell!

It is hard to tell that everytime I fail
    To hate you, for within you "I" dwell
    We will end up like this, I never knew
    I miss you but don't want to see you
    For I don't know how to act
    And how not to react
    When I see you there
    When we stand near
    When my eyes rebel against my mind
    And only you, they try to find
    In every corner, in every place
    Then my heart, that seems in race
    And keeps running with light's speed
    Then I start talking without any need
    My words that don't make any sense
    And I try my best not to make any offense
    For, I don't know what I say or do
    Because all I can see is only you
    Your eyes said so much last time
    I don't know weather that was a sign
    But I never felt that intensity between us before
    May be this is just my illusion once more
    Yet I can't forget my life's that longest day

When every second I tried to stay away
From you, but I failed
Because my eyes confessed
What I was holding inside me
Yet, I let myself to be free
But then it became hard
I couldn't stand there at all
My eyes were busy in finding you
But I wanted to hide everything too
So I don't want to see you again
For it will give me only pain
As I am used to hide and deny
But now I can't, that's why
It is better that our roads may never cross
Because I can't again bear your loss
_ Rubab Tunio

CHAPTER THIRTEEN

What if it hurts?

Aren't you a human being?
    What if it hurts?
    It was always this and not that?
    Bearing pain within my chest,
    I was wondering and loitering thereby the crest.
    What was it that was producing smoke?
    Oh!it was my broken heart turned to wood,
    burning with fire,
    because of unwanted desire,
    broken into pieces producing sparks forming smokes.
    How could you think you could mend it?
    Care and love now doubtful when people around you change so suddenly and unexpectedly.
    World seems a curse when heaven becomes a hell,
    without your beloved around you.
    Somebody snatching ,
    your face purplish and blue.
    Thousands of days is now lost,
    surrounding darkness no moonlight.
    Broken bridges difficult to mend,
    time will take to heal your strength.
    Keep it in mind this is not the end ,
    Somebody is watching you lovingly.

-Darshana Thapa

CHAPTER FOURTEEN

An Afflicted Story

It's a picture of a couple
    Who were supposed to hustle,
    In which one focused on chemistry
    And other was full of mystery.
    To normalize he made numerous sacrifice
    But she never ever compromised,
    Finally he was the one who struggled
    She made his life completely puzzled.
    Suddenly the bond got shattered
    Meanwhile feelings also got scattered,
    For her he was just a toy
    Since she was dating another boy.
    This lad didn't have any other choice
    Also he was unable to listen his voice,
    Still she didn't realise her mistake
    His emotions were got extremely betrayed.
    Every story does not have happy ending
    Loads of people are still suffering,
    So beware and make a wise connection
    Who truly loves you and shows devotion.
    _ Har Deepansh Bahadur Sinha

CHAPTER FIFTEEN

Joyful pain

In the path of true love
    Many got caught in hands of parents
    Not everyone's parents give Green signal
    Majority of them won't accept
    It's happens in mine story
    They do oppose my love
    I don't have a way to communicate him
    After a long struggle, I called him
    The silence and tears while speaking
    Is a huge feel that I can't express in words
    He calm me with pleasant and energetic words
    The longingness to talk
    and to connect each other
    Has been a biggest thinking
    That always striking in mind
    That time,those days
    I also faced the guilty in my heart
    That I had done hatred to my parents
    My hearts in unbalanced pharse
    I need him and I want my parents too
    I can't hurt both
    Days passes,
    unexpected meet up happens sometimes

As we both level up in career
My parents accept my love and him
We both happily married
Leading a lovely life
There has been a pain behind
Every love story.
_ Darshini. M

CHAPTER SIXTEEN

Heavens seems to be cry...!

The heavens seem to be cry ,
    As if something wonderful is dying.
    The thunder rolls .
    The skies tear open .
    Lost dreams and ,
    Wasted wishes falling fast .
    A heart of stone finally turns to ash ,
    Letting taste take over .
    Never knowing what to come .
    Its all part of destiny .
    Just how far will go it up to you ,
    And me the story gets re-written,
    With tears of the angles.
    I'd same you from this hell if i could ,
    Just to get is back to good .
    How many times i have dropped to my knees .
    Telling myself to never let go ,
    And on these lonely nights .
    I try and keep forever in my sights .
    The reminders of you are every where ,
    But I have seen it all,

And still can find u here .
Maybe cause I need you,
But cant feel you .
I don't know what to do,
If all i know is gone ...!
_ Bhumika

CHAPTER SEVENTEEN

The One That Got Away

Remembering the days
 when you played guitar,
 Holding my hand
 in the back of the car.
 Looking at the sun together
 when it set
 Recalling the day,
 in the park we met
 You told me,
 you would never let me go,
 But now you have;
 only let me low
 Playing the guitar,
 while I sang with you
 Now you do the same,
 with someone new.
 I hope you treat her
 right this time,
 while I wait for my heart
 to beat just fine
 Ages have passed

and centuries it might take,
For all my love,
you certainly forsake
For all I know,
I have come to pray,
for you, my dear,
are the one that got away.
_ Diya Roy

CHAPTER EIGHTEEN

A letter to my Love –

If I could pen down a saga of our loveless tale I would weave a dream,
  With all the memories those we have witnessed ,
  And I would fuse it with my verses,
  A hue of melancholic rhythm,
  If you could accompany I would dive deeper into the stream ;
  Of how my untamed spirits jingle all the way,
  And I would say it aloud,
  That I need you to the most to soothe my rude mind,
  But you know my arrogant insight will not ready to confide,
  As it is the only answer to your unheard question,
  But now on I will print my apology in every pamphlet that you would not read...
  _ Sudipta Mishra

CHAPTER NINETEEN

Where I am All Alone

My footsteps lead to the way
    Which is not a bed of roses,
    Where I am all alone,
    Nobody is ready to walk with me,
    Only thorns of criticism are there,
    Hurting me again and again,
    In spite of obstructions,
    Am moving with a hope in my heart,
    That one day these thorns
    Will turn into delicate flowers.
    _ Soniya Sangwan

CHAPTER TWENTY

Red

Something is missing,
    What, I don't know...
    Someone is missing,
    Who, I don't know...
    Something in my heart,
    What, I don't know...
    Perhaps the wet sand,
    Why, I don't know...
    Something is still wet in my
    Heart...
    Are they memories,
    Or the feeling of touching,
    The wet sand with my hands?
    God knows everything...
    Something is still smiling in me...
    Something is still crying in me...
    What is that smile,
    What is that cry,
    I don't know...
    Perhaps,
    A wound is still present in my
    Heart...
    People say,

Time is the best healer,
But I feel as if day by day,
My wound is getting fresher and fresher,
Deeper and Deeper,
So bloody that I am finding myself,
Being reddish just like the colour
Of blood...
Love and Blood,
Both have the same colour Red...
_ Gunjan Jogia

CHAPTER TWENTY-ONE

Yes there is pain in love

Yes there is pain in love
    You have to keep quiet
    When want to speak loud
    You have to suffer
    You have to adjust
    But you should look fine
    Yes there is pain in love
    _ Himanshu Rawat

CHAPTER TWENTY-TWO

I can win every sword

Love is a informal word,
    Which few people like and dislike,
    But it's many people's sword.
    Love yourself wholeheartedly,
    Speak with your heart openheartedly,
    You can win everyone's sword.
    The pain of dejection ,
    The pain of anticipation,
    in my heart kills like a sword.
    With forever longing,
    With forever yearning,
    You are in my heart forever like a sword.
    _ Christy Gnana Deepa J

CHAPTER TWENTY-THREE

Beauty Of The Mother's Love

In the springtime of the year
    The trees wear blossom gown
    With full of fragrance over the sky
    Leaves falling down softly,
    To make a carpet on the ground
    Soon,wind makes leaves whistling
    And send them dancing in the sky.
    Cute small round shaped bird
    Fly Soar through the sky,
    As their light weighted body
    Carry them with wounded features,
    It's time to built a nest of its own
    And find a place to lay some eggs
    Right time is near, after the incubate,
    Look forward for the babies appear,
    Mother bird with wounded wings
    Find uneasy in search of food,
    For the young one in the nest,
    Looking for the food far away
    And feed it to the young one,
    Even make of its stomach empty,

Mother bird safeguard the young one
From various weather condition,
Through spreading the wounded feather
Over the young one,to keep them warm...
There is no place safer than a mother's arm
There is no smile prettier than a mother's smile
There is no greater love than a mother's love..
 _ G.Abarna

CHAPTER TWENTY-FOUR

Pain in Rain

Heavy raindrops are in this early morning.
    The cold breeze touches my skin;
    When I sipped my coffee to warm my soul.
    I heard every single raindrops that falls down in the soil;
    Like a mom hugged her child.
    My heart feels heavy :
    Like the clouds carries the rain.
    The sky is dark again;
    Like the thoughts that covers my brain.
    I hope that the rumbling sound of the thunder
    May be shut it all down.
    But it didn't............!
    I saw the reflection of my tired self in the
    Broken glass of my windows.
    And my heart silently cries in pain.
    The rain races down the window;
    Like the tears falls from my eyes.
    And all I can hear again;
    Is the sound of the heavy rain.
    _ Sujisha Subrahmanian

Introdusing Co-authors

PRAGYA VERMA

Poem: **Unheard Voices**

Pragya Verma hails from Prayagraj, Uttar Pradesh. She is a poetess, writer, author, compiler and co-author. She is the author of 4 anthologies namely, "Shades of Night", "In A Relationship With Success", "Pour out Emotions & "Mist of Words". She has been co-authored in 191+ anthologies, 5+ International anthologies and 17+ World Record anthologies. She pours out her thoughts and emotions through her poetries which heals her and her reader's heart. To read her poetries follow her on Instagram: @wordsofpragya

HARSHITA VERMA

Poem: **BROKEN HEART**

Co-author Harshita Verma is a writer from Lucknow. She has completed her graduation in commerce stream. She has been writing poetry for the last few years as her passion. She wants to be a novelist in future.

Swapna S. Tripathy

Poem: **Need is not Love And Love is not need & My heartbeat says**

Swapna S. Tripathy is pursuing her graduation in horticulture at OUAT. She is inspired from Vijay Deverkonda. She manages her carrier as well as her passion for writing. Her hobbies are scribbling and playing badminton. She is the sparkle star of her family. She's from Bhubaneswar the temple city of Odisha.

Sheena Catherine

Poem: **My Love in Pain...**

Sheena Catherine is a girl who likes to write. She wants to succeed in life by living her own dreams. She is a broad minded person. She wants to do everything in her own ways.

Sakthidevi. J

Poem: UNCONDITIONAL LOVE WITH PAIN

"Fighting for my dreams". I am Sakthidevi completed B.A. English literature, writer @cornucopia_ and participated in anthology of "Beats of Heart" and "Shinning Dreams" and compiled book "The invisible bond".

Anushiya. B

Poem: **Diaries of love**

A literary student filled with full of enthusiasm to learn and to write. She likes to express her inner thoughts and feelings through the flow of words. An individual trying to support and motivate people through her blog https://letusrecreate.blogspot.com/ and also read her quotes through IG @cornucopia_ Co-author of two anthologies "Shining Dreams" and " Beats of Heart". One of the compiler of anthology "The Invisible Bond"

L. Caroline Felicita

Poem: **PAIN IN LOVE**

My name is Caroline Felicita. I'm from TamilNadu. I'm a passionate writer. I have completed MA in Englishliterature. My love for English grow more each and every day. My poems were Published in many anthologies and I write stories in online platform Wattpad they are called as "Only in dreams", "Second coming" and" My dead realtives". I want to achieve more in writing. I Love to write on horror genre. I love dancing and singing too.

Chakshu pahuja

Poem: **Somethings ought to be just loved**

She is Chakshu pahuja ,daughter of Manoj kumar pahuja and Sharda pahuja, her home town is rajpura ,punjab. She is extrovert kind of nature and brings up the topics negelected by the society. She has done 50 anthologies as a coauthor till now and much more to come.

B. NISHANTHINI

Poem: DESOLATED ME

She, B. Nishanthini, born at Erode(dt), Tamilnadu, India- a literature student and a cynophilist love to spend time with her pets. Chasing the footprints of her family by holding hands with her friends to reach a good destination. She believes that literature made a drastic impact in her life. She loves to cherish the taste of English. Writer @cornucopia and co-author of an anthology called "The Invisible Bond". She is a sketch artist and sometimes she practices craft works too. Creativity pulls her that's way now she is a writer...

RUBAB TUNIO

Poem: **It is hard to tell!**

Rubab Tunio is an emerging author from Pakistan who is a poetess, short story writer and co-author of many international anthologies. She is as lively as literature and makes her every minute count. Her love for traveling and deep observation makes her able to see ordinary things in extra ordinary way and it gives birth to new ideas in her mind. She has written more than a hundred poems, many award winning short stories and revolutionary articles that touch almost every genre of literature and universal themes. She believes in the power of pen to awaken ourselves and revolutionize the society.

What she feels, she writes.

Darshana Thapa

Poem: **What if it hurts?**

She is a self published author. She has contributed in many anthologies. She has recently compiled an anthology book 'Unspoken Words'. She is fond of nature and it's beauty. Journey of life is still a mystery for her .She wants to explore it. Learning and gaining knowledge, sharing her thoughts to the society has become her passion.

Har Deepansh Bahadur Sinha

Poem: **AN AFFLICTED STORY**

He is Har Deepansh Bahadur Sinha .He belongs to Lucknow,UP. He has done masters in Geography from National Post Graduate College. Completed his schooling from Study Hall. His hobbies are art, listening to music, cooking & loads of driving. His interest areas are Astronomy, Writing, Photography & Travelling.

Darshini. M

Poem: **Joyful pain**

She is dharshini from kovilpatti. She is pursing masters in English. She has huge interest in writing. She has done many anthology as co-author. She has published a book named "vox of mine".

Bhumika

Poem: **Heavens seems to be cry...!**

Im Bhumika, a bio student . Studying in class 12th . Im not a professional writer but i write poetry to that people feel related and live through it . Poems make me clam and it expresses the felling wich i cannot explain . Writing can be a really personal experience as well as a professional experience and for me its both . I am an national basketball player , state athlete and now a writer . This is my 4th writeup as a co author hope you'll like it .

Thank you .!

DIYA ROY

Poem: **The One That Got Away**

Diya, a seventeen year old who is currently living with her parents while she is preparing to complete high school. You will mostly find her with a book in hand, headphones on, while bobbing her head to Taylor Swift's music.

Sudipta Mishra

Poem: **A letter to my Love** –

Sudipta Mishra is a versatile artist who has excelled in several areas of art and culture. She is a great classical dancer. She has penned down two bestselling books like Superb Express, The Essence of Life. She has been continuously musing in different social platforms like Youth Ki Awaaz, Momspresso, Your Quotes. Currently, she is working as a co-editor of English Magazine: Mouthpiece. Presently, she is residing in Puri with her lovely daughter, Shreeya.

SONIYA SANGWAN

Poem: **WHERE I AM ALL ALONE**

Soniya Sangwan is a published poet who has been the co-author of two books. She belongs to Haryana. She is pursuing her higher studies now and likes to write romantic poetry as well as inspirational poetry.

GUNJAN JOGIA

Poem: **Red**

Gunja Vinodi (Gunjan Jogia) hails from Porbandar, Gujarat. She is the mother of two children. in English literature A graduate, but he loves his mother tongue (Hindi and Gujarati) more. read, write, There is a passion for dance, music and travel. She has written for more than 100 anthologies. their reading His passion has inspired him to write. By adding the name of himself and his father, he automatically to 'Goonja Humor'; Nickname given. She wants her father's name to be immortal in the world by her words.

INTRODUSING CO-AUTHORS

HIMANSHU RAWAT

Poem: **Yes there is pain in love**

Parents put his name as Himanshu Rawat. But he called himself as shayar_bychance. Yes its his insta id and passion too. Currently pays electricity bill of a house in Chandigarh. Like other millions of people he is also college going student who is pursuing B.Com. Enthusiasm and positive minded are his qualities. A true human who loves to help people. His motto of life is to learn and explore as much as he can

Christy Gnana Deepa J

Poem: **I can win every sword**

Christy Gnana Deepa, hailing from Tamilnadu, India and now residing in Madurai for her studies.Her journey till date is amazing by being a compiler of 6 anthologies and a co-author of more than 50 anthologies. A writer by passion and a literarian by profession. She posts her writeups on Yourquote, Instagram and NbliK. You can follow her on instagram

(___budding___writer) for more writeups

G.ABARNA

Poem: **BEAUTY OF THE MOTHER'S LOVE**

A student of literature, who is a cynophilist, very much fond of dogs and in gardening. Watching K dramas make me feel better so it can be said that I am addicted to it! My favourite hobby is to spread smiles and warmth everywhere!! JUST BE HAPPY THAT'S IT.......

Compiler

SUJISHA SUBRAHMANIAN

Sujisha Subrahmanian, daughter of Mr. Subrahmanian and Mrs. Siji Subrahmanian, from Thrissur, Kerala. She has completed her Post Graduation in English Literature and started her career as a writer. Currently she focused on her MPhil. She believes in staying happy with whatever she has and also believes the fact that 'if you not follow your heart, you've not the right to spend the rest of your life wishing you had'. Her favourites include reading, music, watching movies and TV shows, going out with her sister, exploring places and living with her loved ones. She had worked in various anthologies and achieved lot of appreciation for her writings.

To know more, follow her on Instagram under the ID @author_sujisha. You are free to mail her at nssujisha@gmail.com. And also look her blog page www.sujishawrites.blog.com.

BOOKS: " Oath of Love", " Beats of Hearts", " Shining Dreams", " Heading your Bets", Tranquil Little Hearts", " Little Colors of Life", Secluded Hearts", Breath & Believe", Those Faded Days", " Flipped", " The Aedents Hearets" & " Thorny Roses".

All are available in Notionpress & Amazon

www.ingramcontent.com/pod-product-compliance
Lightning Source LLC
LaVergne TN
LVHW091934070526
838200LV00068B/1164